Listing Life

Easy list-making to discover who
you really are, what you truly want
from life & how to get it

Amy Doak

www.listinglife.com.au

Copyright © 2021

All rights reserved. No part of this publication may be reproduced, stored in a retrieval system or transmitted in any form by any means without the prior permission of the copyright owner. Enquiries should be made to the publisher.

Every effort has been made to ensure that this book is free from error or omissions. However, the Publisher, the Author, the Editor or their respective employees or agents, shall not accept responsibility for injury, loss or damage occasioned to any person acting or refraining from action as a result of material in this book whether or not such injury, loss or damage is in any way due to any negligent act or omission, breach of duty or default on the part of the Publisher, the Author, the Editor, or their respective employees or agents.

The Author, the Publisher, the Editor and their respective employees or agents do not accept any responsibility for the actions of any person - actions which are related in any way to information contained in this book.

The moral right of the author has been asserted.

A CIP catalogue record of this book is available from the National Library of Australia.

Author: Doak, Amy

Title: Listing Life: Easy list-making to discover who you really are, what you truly want from life & how to get it

ISBN: 9781925900026 (Paperback)

Subject: Personal Improvement, Self Help, Life Coaching

Dewey Number: 158.1

Cover abstract art by Freeject.net; internal abstract art by Basia Stryjecka; watercolour images by Beehouse Design Studio. The publisher has done its utmost to attribute the copyright holders of all the visual material used. If you nevertheless think that a copyright has been infringed, please contact the publisher.

Published by:
Fiosracht Press (an imprint of Of The World Publishing)
ACN 133 333 141
PO Box 8070
Bendigo South LPO VIC 3550
AUSTRALIA

www.oftheworldbooks.com

Fiosracht Press

"To know what you prefer, instead of humbly saying Amen to what the world tells you you ought to prefer, is to have kept your soul alive."

- Robert Louis Stevenson

"It is not about 'finding yourself', it's about creating yourself. Stop complaining and get to work."

- Jim Carrey

Contents

	Page
Introduction	7
Part 1: Who are you?	13
Part 2: What brings you joy?	39
Part 3: What do you want?	53
Part 4: How do you get what you want?	71
Part 5: Your resources	85

Introduction

What's this all about?

It's complicated, isn't it? This whole LIFE thing. And everyone expects so much from you.

From a very early age, we are asked 'what do you want to be when you grow up?' Of course, no one expects a five-year-old to offer little more than a cute anecdote, but the five-year-old doesn't know that. Then the five-year-old grows up to become a high school student and suddenly the question takes on more weight. After all, it's at about the age of 16 that most people are asked to choose a discipline that will lead them through their senior years of school and on to Further Study and eventually A Career. Scary stuff.

If it helps, I will turn 45 soon and I still don't really know what I am going to be when I grow up. I'm very happy with that though, and I've got lots of lovely plans to fill in the time between Now and whenever The End arrives. What I have learnt (the hard, long and windy way) is that it's less about what you Name It and more about how you spend your time.

Annie Dillard, in her book 'The Writing Life', famously wrote: "how we spend our days is of course how we spend our lives. What we do with this hour and that one is what we are doing." She was referring to scheduling writing time when she wrote this, but it's relevant enough to most of us that the words are universally known. The truth is, once enough time has passed and we look back, we do indeed realise that all those moments when we were waiting for our Life to begin was, in fact, our Actual Life.

It's incredibly easy to fill those hours and those days with the wants and needs of those around us. I'm sure many good people have done just that and perhaps even been happy doing so. Of course, if you're like me, then there may just be a little voice in the back of your mind saying, "there's more than this, isn't there?"

Maybe. Maybe not. Maybe you think you want things that you actually don't.

I'm skipping ahead though.

Here's the thing: I truly believe that we all know who we are. As we get older and take on more responsibilities, it's easy to get caught up in other people's projections and perceptions, not to mention all those societal 'shoulds', and it's easy to lose who touch with the real you. What we focus on becomes our truth and the other bits, the real us, gets pushed aside.

I like to refer to it as our internal Whoville. Stay with me here. I'm not completely bonkers (I don't think). In the Dr. Seuss book 'Horton Hears A Who', we meet a caring and thoughtful elephant (Horton) who one day hears shouting from the end of a dandelion about to take flight. It's an entire world you see (Whoville), and they're about to be swept away in the wind, until Horton hears their cries and vows to save them. All the other animals in the jungle think Horton is mad, but he stays true to what he hears ("I'll just have to save him because, after all, a person's a person, no matter how small") and (spoiler) he does indeed save Whoville.

I like to think we get about like Horton: busy taking our place in the jungle of life. Until one day we hear a desperate voice shouting out for us. The one, deep down inside, that is looking for validation, attention and a chance to thrive. The one we stopped paying attention to long ago. It may start small, but if you ignore it, it will get louder and more insistent.

I believe that if we can save our very own Whoville, work out who that voice belongs to and what they need to thrive, then we will have uncovered our sense of purpose and joy.

And for such a seemingly complicated task, I have employed a very simple solution.

Lists.

You might associate lists with a visit to the grocery store. Or a to-do list that sits on your desk or kitchen bench with items that get moved from one day to the next as we procrastinate our way through life waiting for the next external deadline (no? Just me then?). However, I promise you, these are not those sort of lists. These are relatively easy lists. Lists that will remind you of the things that make you uniquely you. The things that bring you joy. The things that you offer to the world, and the things that, if undertaken, will ensure that the way you spend your days (and, in turn, your life) will be filled with all that is good and wonderful.

These exercises are about tapping into the good and discovering how you can make that part of your every day.

If you're the rebellious type, who gets bored easily and doesn't like being told what to do, then know you don't have to create these lists in the order they've been presented. It might help your brain connect the dots a little easier if you do, but I appreciate that everyone's brain works differently so your first exercise is to just go with what feels right. Start in the middle if it pleases you. You might find that a single exercise unlocks exactly what you needed or were looking for (if so, lucky you).

You may also find yourself getting a little judgmental as you progress ('that sounds silly', 'who am I to be thinking that', 'people would think that is so boring') and to that I say SHHHH! The negative voices in your head don't get a say in much of this process (there's a few opportunities though, so tell them to wait their turn and if they are good and keep quiet you might give them a say).

Many of these lists will require you to (rather than listen to the negative—which are so often other people's voices anyway) pay attention to your little, quiet Whoville. We're going to give them a voice before they blow away in the wind on the end of a dandelion forever.

This book is broken into five sections (well, six if you include this part here, and I don't. In fact, I find lots of people don't even read introductions so thank you if you've made it this far).

Part 1 is a reminder of who you really, truly are. I'm sure you've forgotten. We all do. It's about recognising that perhaps the things we think we want, or the things we think we should want, aren't necessarily what we are seeking at all.

Part 2 is all about the things that bring us joy. Remember that feeling? Joy. It seems to get further and further out of our grasp as we get older, which is silly really because you'd think over time we would get better at knowing where to find it. The thing is, if you are a little more aware about what brings you joy (and your list will be unique to you) then you're more likely to ensure that those things become a part of your everyday. Doesn't that sound nice? Having joyful moments everyday? It can be done!

Part 3 is learning to put Parts 1 and 2 in to perspective in order to determine what you want out of this one life that you have been given. The iconic performer, Madonna, was quoted as saying: "A lot of people don't get what they want, that's because they don't ask for what they want." Which is very true. The rub is, it's hard to say what you want if you don't actually know what that is. Understanding what you really want is a challenge unto itself. Thankfully, there are lists for that.

Part 4 will ensure that you don't just stop with the knowing. Once you've figured out what needs to be done to bring the joy into your life, then you need to learn how to make that happen. Decision making and goal setting sounds really hard and boring, but actually, it's quite simple. And, once you've done it, you just get to go about your life. Your Whoville will be sure to happily take over once they know what to do.

Finally, Part 5 looks, at first glance, like a heap of empty pages. They're for you though. Once you've tackled Parts 1 through 4, you'll have more of an idea of what to put in your Joy Bucket. And you'll start collecting those things. So the pages in Part 5 are for you to make a note of what you find.

This is a book to be carted about and scribbled in and then popped somewhere you can easily revisit it when you feel like the voices of Whoville are starting to sound tinny and echo-y and far away. Many of these questions I started asking and answering in my mid-20s. It was surprising (and not-so) to find that 20 years later I was actually on the right track all along.

The thing is, as well as clearly being a slow learner, I missed a few valuable steps in the process. Now that I've figured them out, I thought it was time to share. Afterall, shouldn't everyone feel as though they are truly themselves? That their days (and nights even) are filled with joy and contentment? That the way they've spent their lives is exactly how it was intended.

Enough lofty promises. Away we go.

Part 1

Who are you?

Before the world got its hands on you (parents, siblings, friends, peers, teachers, extended family and popular culture) you knew exactly who you were.

You only have to meet a newborn baby and pay attention to recognise that we arrive on this earth with a solid sense of self.

Genetics, gender, environment and other constraints aside, the truth of a human's interests and qualities actually emerge fairly quickly. The kid who is constantly on the move and bouncing balls; the kid who is fascinated by bugs; the one who dances from room to room on tip toes; the child who knows the name, make and model of every truck, car and tractor; the kid who paints and draws on every available surface... including themselves.

Now this isn't to say that that your childhood obsession is your perfect career choice—you haven't just witnessed a footballer, a scientist, a dancer, an auto engineer or an artist in the making. What you have seen though, is the activity that brings that little human great joy.

Often, as the human gets older they are told their interest is childish, or boring, or nerdy, or stupid. Sometimes they're told it's a 'waste of time' because it's seemingly an activity that can't be monetised (which is rubbish actually, because just about everything can be monetised these days).

As a child, you spend a fair chunk of time being bored and it seems that boredom triggers your mind and body to explore your interests. Have a think about what you gravitated to when you were young. If you can't think of anything, talk to your family members and see what memories they have of you when you were little.

With those activities coming in to your awareness, remember how those things made you feel. Remember how they filled your heart up and made time disappear—just like magic—and how you didn't care at all about what else was happening in the world when you were immersed in that? It was just you, in the moment.

What did you love as a child?

List six things that you were passionate about when you were small (dolls, trucks, singing, dancing, balls, sports, books, collecting, crafting, the outdoors):

1.

2.

3.

4.

5.

6.

Ooohh... this is a tricky one, isn't it? Don't want to get too big for our boots, right? Who are you to be thinking you're good at stuff anyway?

If you didn't read the introduction (or perhaps you've forgotten already) I specifically requested the negative voices SHHH. It's not their turn yet.

So tell me, what are you good at? Can you make a fantastic chocolate cake? Maybe you tell great jokes? Or you're good at putting others at ease? Perhaps you can solve a Rubicks cube in under a minute? Or stand in lines for hours on end and not get bored or annoyed? Or remember all the lyrics to every song in the Top 10 singles of 1991?

Think outside the box and be as obscure as you like. Complimenting yourself takes practice and time when you're not used to it, but it does get easier.

If you're really struggling, ask a friend or family member: "what do you think I'm good at?" Don't worry if they screw up their face and can't think of anything right away. Others, you see, are so used to thinking about themselves all the time, it takes a shift in their brain to focus on someone else (this is a very important fact to remember whenever you think everyone is thinking about you and focusing on you...they're not. They're much too self-obsessed for that). Wait patiently with an expectant face and they will come up with an answer or two.

Of course, it's especially nice if you can come up with your own answers. Being aware of your strengths as well as your weaknesses is very handy. That pesky 'negative bias' we all have is often ready to take the lead. Remember the good stuff too.

Being good at things is just one part of the puzzle though. Actually enjoying the thing you're good at is the most wonderful feeling (and, alongside that, just because you're good at something, doesn't mean you should do that thing). So, once you've listed 10, I'd then like to think about which of those brings you great joy.

What are you good at?

List ten things that you know you are quite good at (ask for help from loved ones if you find this exercise a bit tricky), then circle the three that make you the happiest:

1.

2.

3.

4.

5.

6.

7.

8.

9.

10.

It's hard to have a hobby or an interest in the current environment, don't you think?

Thanks to Instagram and Etsy and everything in between, if you dare even hint at trying something new or tackling a new interest, you're likely to be bombarded with "oh, that could be a business!" or, "you should put that online, people might buy that".

I've even been guilty of offering the same advice (sorry, all of you).

The thing is, this intense need to monetise pretty much everything we do causes two big problems.

The first is, it makes us feel guilty for every single activity that isn't 'achieving'. If you're not making money, or serving another, or making yourself look a certain way, then clearly it's a waste of time. So we're told.

The second is, we're not allowed to be bad at anything, because we're somehow supposed to make every passing interest our Next Big Thing.

Stop it.

Immediately.

Have a think about what you might be interested in, just a passing curiosity is enough. It could be early 20th century photography; global politics; meditation; propagating plants; brewing beer; crocheting teeny tiny woodland animals.

If you didn't have to be good at those things, or make money from them, or sign up for a course so one day you can teach that thing . . . what might you delve in and out of? What might you discover more about if the pressure was taken off a little?

What are you curious about?

List six things that spark your interest (remember, you don't have to become an expert at these, you just might be curious to learn more about them):

1.

2.

3.

4.

5.

6.

Another thing we tend to stop doing early in life is moving our body just for the sheer feel of it.

Someone tells us that's being silly. Someone else says you're doing it wrong. Before we know it, we've stopped altogether. Then, in an attempt to get 'fit and healthy' the moving we do becomes more like torture than pleasure.

Do you remember that episode of the TV show Friends when Phoebe and Rachel went running together and Phoebe's running style was arms and legs everywhere? Rachel was so embarrassed that she tried to make excuses to not run with her. Finally, Phoebe was able to explain that running that way was fun for her—that's what made the experience enjoyable. She didn't care if someone thought she looked crazy—she was gone before they even really noticed. Rachel gave it a go and realised her friend was right. It was fun.

I'm not saying that you need to go for a run with your arms and legs flying (but you can if you want). Rather, I'd like you to think about ways that you moved your body in the past that were enjoyable.

It's not just the movement that will bring you joy, it's the surrounding conditions that make all the difference.

Maybe you enjoy a leisurely stroll somewhere pretty, or perhaps you like to put on your favourite music and dance 'til you're red and sweaty while you sing loudly into a hairbrush microphone? Do you love to immerse yourself in cold water? Or ride a bike through the bush feeling the jolt of the dirt beneath the wheels?

What about swinging as high as you can on a swing? Climbing a tree? Jumping on a trampoline?

When you've made your list of four things, and hopefully each makes you smile at the thought, ask yourself the question: when was the last time I did that? It might be time to give it another go.

You won't be moving for calorie expenditure, or because 'you should', you'll be doing it just because it makes you feel good. What a novel idea!

How do you love to move?

List four ways that you enjoy moving your body (dancing, walking, running, cycling, swimming, etc)—get specific about what that looks like:

1.

2.

3.

4.

When, do you suppose, did you lose confidence in your ability to be the master of your life? To make things happen and to deal with any issue that comes your way?

Sometimes people have such a rough trot that they simply stop out of pure exhaustion. Other times, there are those who have been berated and put down for trying things, so they stop for fear of judgement. Then there are the ones who have inherited their fear of a challenge, after being told that some things just aren't possible.

As it turns out, anything and everything is possible. There are literally thousands of examples out there where people have actually accomplished the very thing they were told they couldn't.

But we're not talking about everyone else here. We are talking about you, and your special set of unique abilities.

I'd like you to cast your mind back and think of instances in your past when stuff has been hard or incredibly challenging. What was the situation? And what did you do in order to handle it, fix it or make it work? Was there a skill you had that was put in to practice? Perhaps one that you didn't even know you had?

Did you have more confidence than you imagined? Did you know more than you thought? Maybe you were cleverer or more innovative than you'd previously given yourself credit for?

It might have been a simple, childhood problem that you can easily see your way out of now, but at the time it would have felt very important. Think of work, home, relationships...and then write down three.

What was the problem? How did you deal with it, and what special skill of yours was uncovered in the process?

When have you handled a tricky situation?

Not just when, but also how—list four instances in your life so far when things were tough and you managed to deal with it:

1.

2.

3.

4.

A favourite quote of mine is accredited to spiritual and meditation teacher, Allan Lokos: "Don't believe everything you think. Thoughts are just that - thoughts."

Writer and teacher, Byron Katie, further expanded this concept with 'The Work' - four questions you need to ask yourself when you're having unhelpful thoughts (you know the ones, those ones that spiral inside your brain and take up all your time and energy):

- is it true?
- can you absolutely know it is true?
- what happens when you believe that thought?
- who would you be without that thought?

These questions, along with Allan Lokos' quote, attempt to remind us that the things we tell ourselves are not the truth. They are simply things we say. Once we've said something to ourselves often enough, we start to accept it as an absolute truth.

In the introduction (and again on page 16) I said that I'd give the negative voices in your head a chance to have their say. This is their shining moment! Have a think about the chatter that often comes up inside your mind...

"I can't do that." "I'm no good at that." "I'm not smart/pretty/talented enough." "I wouldn't know what to do/say."

I could go on, but it seems to be the case with humans that we are very, very good at making ourselves feel bad without the help of others. So go ahead. What statements do you regularly berate yourself with?

When you're done (and I sincerely hope this exercise wasn't too easy for you), there are two things I want you to consider:

- Has that statement originated from somewhere else (can you place the words in someone else's mouth... perhaps a peer, family member or teacher? And if you can, make a note of who initially said that 'truth').

- Secondly, is it true? Really, absolutely? I'm going to guess that it isn't, but even if you don't believe me, I want you to hold that question in your mind for each time you say those words. You might discover, eventually, that I am correct.

What are the nice things?

What compliments have you been given over the years that have made you feel good about yourself? List four, and be sure to note who said it:

1.

2.

3.

4.

Happiness is such a funny word. The official, Oxford, definition is: 'feeling or showing pleasure or contentment', but it seems to mean different things to different people.

In this instance, I think we need to stick with the Oxford meaning. Feeling pleasure or contentment.

In the next section, we're going to go into a bit more detail about how to capture this feeling, but for now I want you to go back in time again. Back to when you were younger and when the things that offered you pleasure were quite simple.

I think most people can relate to a moment of finding, or being given money, and then going to a store to spend that unexpected windfall on something sweet.

One of my greatest childhood memories was our family holiday. We always spent a few weeks in late spring at the beach and even all these years later I find that mild days, cool nights, soft sand, salty air and ocean waves give me immense pleasure.

So now I want you to step away from the negativity on the previous page and think about moments, however brief, that made you feel truly happy and content.

When you recall that moment, do so with all your senses. What was it about the sounds, smells, sights or feelings that made those moments so blissful for you?

As a side note, do you know what is so wonderful about writing down these moments?

Time, when you really pull it apart, is a construct that humans have created to systemise their lives. The past doesn't exist outside of our retelling of it and the future will never actually arrive (it's always in the future!) so what you do with the details of what happened before now is actually completely up to you. Good, joyful memories are nice to shelve in a happy box. They remind us of good times, but they also help us recognise why we enjoy certain things today.

When did you feel truly happy?

List five instances when you felt joyful, blissful, happy or content—even fleeting ones count, and be specific:

1.

2.

3.

4.

5.

Have you ever thought about the legacy that you will leave behind?

I'm not talking about children, or money, or property, but more about how you would like to be remembered.

Whether this is after you've lived a long and happy life, or after you've left a room full of friends or strangers, what would you like people to say about you when you're gone?

There are three parts to this exercise, mainly because people are far too polite and conservative when it comes to anticipating their own impact.

On the page opposite, I'd like you to list five things that you'd like to be remembered for after you're gone.

Have you done that? Good.

Now, if you're like most people, you've probably written things like 'kind' or 'loving partner or parent' or 'thoughtful'. Which is all very well and good, but it's a little generic, don't you think? On the second list, over the page, I want you to try again. This time, I want you to be a bit silly. If you could really be remembered for something in generations to come, what might it be? Being a cutting edge and dynamic conservationist and environmentalist? Acting in a movie? Writing a book? Inventing something? Winning a Nobel Peace Prize?

Maybe your vision of glory is closer to home. Responsible for the amazing family cookie recipe? Quilted the rug that was passed down through generations? Started the family business?

Have fun with it and just see what your subconscious comes up with.

Finally, with the last list, meet somewhere in the middle. If kind and loving is truly all you want to be remembered for, that is a noble response. It also means that your life can be very, very simple from here on in, because they're pretty straightforward goals that can be actioned immediately.

Regardless, perhaps it's time to start living in the sort of way that you want to be remembered. No better time to start than right now.

How do you want to be remembered?

If you were to die having lived a long life, list five things you'd like people to say about you at your funeral:

1.

2.

3.

4.

5.

What might be a fun way to be remembered?

In your wildest imagination, in a world where anything is possible, list five things you'd like people to say about you at your funeral:

1.

2.

3.

4.

5.

How do you really, truly want to be remembered?

Now get honest: list five things you'd like people to say about you at your funeral if you had lived your dream life:

1.

2.

3.

4.

5.

By now, I'm hoping that you are feeling a little more like yourself. You're remembering what it feels like to be you—rather than the person you think you need to be.

A great way to really determine what is important, is to uncover your values. Your values are the things that matter most to you and everyone has different values. Often, the reason someone else might rub us the wrong way, is because what is important to them isn't important to us, and vice versa. Someone having different values to you doesn't make them wrong and you right, it just makes you both unique.

Your priority may be security and responsibility, someone else may feel that freedom and playfulness are more important. This can cause issues in the dynamic (especially if you're two people trying to work on a project together, or co-parent children) but it doesn't make either of you bad people.

Recognising your own values allows you to understand what makes you tick and why certain people, places and projects resonate with you more than others.

Even better, when you've established what your values are, it can help greatly in decision-making. Perhaps you've been offered a job in a quiet office where you don't interact with many people, but community is one of your core values. Knowing this will help you understand that this job will not be satisfactory in the long-term.

This list is not at all exhaustive and you may even want to add to it. However, first I need you to circle every word that feels good and positive to you.

Over the next page, you need to shortlist your choices. This doesn't mean the things you are disregarding aren't important to you—it simply means that something else is more important.

The other thing to note during this exercise is that it might be tempting to circle the things you think you should value. Don't do it. No one needs to see this list aside from you, so get selfish and get really honest with yourself. You might be surprised by what you come up with.

What are your core values?

Circle everything on the list below that is very important to you (try your hardest not to circle everything but add your own if need be, prioritise!):

Independence	Authenticity	Integrity
Courage	Creativity	Responsibility
Achievement	Competitiveness	Logic
Fun	Enthusiasm	Accountability
Adaptability	Compassion	Justice
Wisdom	Healing	Joy
Diligence	Community	Inner peace
Wealth	Tranquillity	Common sense
Trust	Control	Morality
Acceptance	Abundance	Sacrifice
Sharing	Inner beauty	Self awareness
Self discipline	Contributing	Making a difference
Flexibility	Diversity	Perseverance
Comfort	Democracy	Passion
Health	Curiosity	Positivity
Image	Forgiveness	Playfulness
Being liked	Influence	Open minded
Balance	Connectedness	Order
Ambition	Financial security	Knowledge
Faith	Efficiency	Loyalty
Future generations	Authority	Success
Global perspective	Emotional wellbeing	Status
Fairness	Empathy	Peace
Change and variety	Hard working	Stability
Productivity	Freedom	Tradition
Adventure	Personal safety	Learning
Respect	Physical wellbeing	Humility
Inspiring others	Gratitude	Humour
Recognition	Honesty	Transparency
Security	Helping others	Harmony

What is your values shortlist?

Choose your favourite ten from the circled list on the previous page and write them below:

1.

2.

3.

4.

5.

6.

7.

8.

9.

10.

What is your values shortlist?

Now choose your top three and write them below. Remember, this list isn't set in stone, your values will evolve and change as you do:

1.

2.

3.

Part 2

What brings you joy?

Righteo then. Now we are up to the fun part. This is the section where we get to think about all the wonderful stuff.

To be fair, it makes sense that everyone wants their life to be a certain way, but we also have to admit that sometimes things don't always turn out the way we expect.

That's OK.

I know, I know. Not what you wanted to hear. This is a book about finding out what you want and then getting what you want, right?

Sort of.

You see, sometimes the things that don't seem to go our way have a habit of actually going our way.

Maybe you didn't get that job you desperately wanted, but that meant you didn't move, and then you met the love of your life at the supermarket.

Maybe the love of your life didn't turn out to be the love of your life, but the child you had with them did.

Maybe the course you studied didn't lead anywhere, but the friends you made or the skills you learnt helped you or brought you joy in other ways.

Maybe the trip that was cancelled allowed you to take another trip, to a different place, that was unexpectedly wonderful.

Do you see where I'm headed here?

I'd like you to list a few ways that life-not-working-out-for-you actually worked out for you.

Those times when you were a bit cross or perhaps just a bit disappointed because the picture you held in your mind didn't quite pan out that way.

Taking in to consideration that if things didn't happen exactly that way, in that moment, then you wouldn't be exactly where you are right now ... what are some instances that have turned out for the best?

What worked out for the best?

List five things that weren't exactly what you wanted but, in hindsight, made your life turn out for the very best:

1.

2.

3.

4.

5.

This next list is a tricky one. Certainly not as easy as you may first think.

10, or even 20 things, is easy. Blue skies. A hug from a loved one. Your favourite song on the radio. However, you'll soon find that it starts getting harder.

We are all so used to seeing the negative in things, sometimes it can be hard to remember the simple things that bring us joy.

The thing is, even saying 'lifting my spirit' makes you inhale and breathe a little deeper, don't you think?

When I first did this exercise, I was very much looking at things —even things that once gave me pleasure—as hard and negative. A few challenges in a row had made me frightened to open myself up to the world. It all just seemed too difficult really.

This list was to (initially) serve as a reminder that there were loads of things that gave me pleasure. Interestingly, other things became apparent too.

First of all, there were a few things that I almost found myself internally apologising for as I wrote them down. I was saying to myself, 'I know this isn't very exciting but . . .' or 'I know other people think this is silly but . . .'

Goodness me. It was MY list, after all. What this told me though, is there were a few things that brought me joy and I was denying myself those things because of other people's opinions. That needed to stop immediately.

The second thing I saw was a pattern. There were certain things that you could definitely group in to a single 'thing' (a lifestyle, a climate, an occupation) and that was very exciting.

After spending such a long time lamenting that I didn't know what to do with this life of mine, it was suddenly abundantly clear that there was lots I could do.

And, bonus, I could really enjoy doing them.

So, take your time and be honest. Think of smells, sounds, flavours, the way things feel. The things that make you feel at home, the things that make you feel safe, the things that— when you think of them—the curl of a smile reaches your face before you have time to register it.

What lifts your spirit?

List 50 things that make you feel light, happy or joyful. Use all your senses and the little things count!

1.

2.

3.

4.

5.

6.

7.

8.

9.

10.

11.

12.

13.
14.
15.
16.
17.
18.
19.
20.
21.
22.
23.
24.
25.
26.
27.
28.
29.
30.
31.

32.
33.
34.
35.
36.
37.
38.
39.
40.
41.
42.
43.
44.
45.
46.
47.
48.
49.
50.

❡ If you have ever encountered a self-help book or speaker, or met someone who speaks of positivity as a practice, one of the little 'tricks' they will offer is this one—gratitude.

Don't roll your eyes at me. There's a reason it works. There's actual science behind it, it seems.

Gratitude enhances empathy and reduces aggression; it helps people relish good experiences; it provides a tool to deal with adversity; it improves self-esteem; it helps you sleep better; it reinforces generous behaviour; it doesn't allow us to take things for granted; it helps you build stronger relationships; and it offers proven psychological, physiological and physical health. So there you go.

If you want to get even more science-y on the gratitude bandwagon, there have been a number of studies showing that a regular practice of gratitude provides a surge of our feel-good chemicals—serotonin, dopamine and oxytocin, and a feeling of stress-free reward in our pre-frontal cortex. These are things people pay good money for in both legal and non-legal drugs and you can actually get it here for free.

Many therapists will tell you to think of five things you're grateful for before bed each night as a support for dealing with anxiety or depression. I think that's a great habit to have, so maybe there's an added list for you once you're done here?

For now, I want you to list 24 things.

Feel free to start small. Running water. Electricity. Food in the fridge. A warm blanket. These might seem silly and inconsequential, but the fact is, most of the world's population do not have such luxuries. And, if you're adding things like 'people who love you' or 'a satisfying job' or 'a holiday to somewhere amazing' then you're really kicking goals.

It's OK to have a lot and still feel a bit shit, that's being human. However, it's also important to remember that you actually do have a lot, and to not take that fact for granted.

Apparently it helps in lots of ways (see paragraph three).

What are you grateful for?

List 24 things that you have in your life that you know you are grateful for (big or small!):

1.

2.

3.

4.

5.

6.

7.

8.

9.

10.

11.

12.

13.

14.

15.

16.

17.

18.

19.

20.

21.

22.

23.

24.

Comparison is the thief of joy, so said US President Theodore Roosevelt. It's true too. Right up there with a saying that's even more common: 'the grass is always greener'.

We have a terrible tendency to look at other people and think they've got it so much better. More money, happier relationships, better jobs, better bodies, an easier life.

It's not true though. They don't. Also, they're possibly looking at you and finding envy in a thing you are completely unaware of. Isn't life a funny thing?

The other stupid thing we tend to do is look at others and criticise. 'I wouldn't raise my children that way.' Or, 'if I had her money I would spend it differently'. Or, 'he gets on my nerves when he talks about XYZ'. Judgey wudgey was a bear, indeed.

There's a theory that the thing we dislike in other people is actually the thing we dislike in ourselves. Seeing it flaunted so openly makes us uncomfortable and annoyed, apparently.

Whether this is accurate or not is not of importance today though. Right now, I'd like you to use your critical eye for a much healthier activity, if you don't mind.

Think of the people you envy or admire. They can be people you know in person, and people you don't. They can happily stay on the pedestal you've got them on, but I would like you to consider exactly what it is about them that makes them so admirable.

Are they generous with their time? Their money? Are they especially intelligent? Do they make you feel wonderful when you've been in their presence? Are they living or working in a way that seems especially nice?

After you've made your list, have a good hard look at those attributes. Do they align with your values (from page 35)? Are they really that special? Are they qualities that you aspire to, or would one day hope to have? If so, are they achievable?

Sometimes envy and comparison can be used for motivation, sometimes it can be slightly shifted to turn to admiration, and sometimes being specific about those qualities can make you realise that you're not so far away from an excellent person after all.

Who do you most admire?

List five people who have traits you admire—they can be people you know personally, or perhaps well-known people who inspire you. List the traits as well as the person:

1.

2.

3.

4.

5.

Part 3

What do you want?

Discovering what you want in life is all well and good, but an excellent way to figure it out is via a process of elimination.

Let's say you've always wanted lots of money, and felt rather dissatisfied with your current lot because, frankly, it's just not enough money.

How much do you really want though? Do you want five houses that require rates and bills paid and ongoing upkeep? Do you want a helicopter and multiple cars that also require work (or staff)? Do you want a house cleaner, a gardener, a chef and a hair stylist ... all of whom require ongoing management? Or do you actually quite like the house you live in, but you'd just like it paid off and enough money to cover the bills when they come in?

And do you really want to live by the sea, in warm weather? Or does sand in everything actually annoy you? And does humid weather create mould and frizzy hair, and in actual fact you'd just prefer a holiday once a year in the dry season?

Do you actually want a job that provides lots of networking lunches and invites to fancy parties? Or is the truth of it that people make you a bit tired and you'd rather be home on the couch with your dog watching TV of an evening?

It's very easy to look at lives-that-aren't-yours and think they're superior in some way. To feel envy and discontent because other people are living what you think is your dream. But is it really, truly your dream?

Have a think about what you've said about alternative lives previously and re-think it with the perspective you've gained from the previous two sections of this book. Do they really sound as wonderful as you thought? Or is there a slight crack in that perfect facade?

Make a list of some seemingly perfect life options that, when you really think about, don't suit you.

When you're done, keep this list in mind. Suddenly, you've got quite a few things that you no longer need to concern yourself with. What freedom!

What sort of life don't you want?

List six things that don't appeal to you in the least (city living, beach living, surrounded by lots of people, or not? What sounds like not-so-much-fun?):

1.

2.

3.

4.

5.

6.

"I know I've said it earlier, but I am going to say it again (and again)—we are all different and we all enjoy different things.

Isn't that marvellous?

It's what makes this world varied and interesting and also one of the many things that makes each of us unique.

Yet, we find ourselves comparing, and ultimately striving, for a lifestyle that is very likely to not appeal to us. Many businesses actually count on that fact and the entire marketing and advertising industry is built on the knowledge that we are very easily fooled in to wanting things that we don't actually even want.

Don't feel bad. People study and work for years to find new and clever ways to trick you into desiring.

Because of this, we spend an awful lot of time coveting homes (and bank balances, and wardrobes, and bodies, and relationships) that perhaps we don't really want. We've somehow fallen in to the trap of believing that if we had those things, we'd be happy. We'd be better versions of ourselves, and we'd never want for another thing ever, ever again.

I can't convince you that it's all a load of rubbish. I can't tell you those things would make you happy for one moment and then you'd be you with your thoughts again and you'd simply move the bar to another wishful-quick-fix. I can't tell you that, because you wouldn't believe me even if I did.

So instead, I will keep your mind busy with another task. I want you to imagine your dream home (fancy, or not) and I want you to think about specific details that would bring you joy. Timber benchtops; or lush, carpeted flooring; or a big garden filled with flowers; or a gorgeous view.

If you love the idea of large oven to cook in, but you currently live somewhere that has a kitchen so small there's no room for even a microwave, that's very telling. The same as dreaming for a huge, spacious kitchen and butler's pantry when you actually hate cooking and would never spend time in the kitchen at all.

Be honest with yourself, what little details exist in your imaginary dream home?

Where would you love to live?

List six elements your 'dream' home has (provide as much detail as possible):

1.

2.

3.

4.

5.

6.

Everyone has perhaps said it before—even if it was a flippant comment: "if I had xx months/days/years to live, I'd really want to do this."

If you've ever been unfortunate enough to be close to someone who has suffered a terminal diagnosis, you might have watched them suffer through that exact dilemma. Sadly, sick people aren't exactly in the mood for great, life-changing moments when the end is near.

So I am going to ask that question of you right now, whilst you still do have some energy about you.

What would you regret, if you found out you were dying and you hadn't yet lived?

What would you wish you'd tried or experienced? Where would you like to have visited? What conversations would you have wanted?

I'm not asking this to be morbid. It's a genuine curiosity. It's quite easy to say you'll 'one day' do this, and 'some day' do that, but those sort of statements assume that one day or some day will actually arrive.

What if they don't?

What if, you were given news that your time was almost up.

What would you absolutely love to achieve before that happened? What don't you want to miss out on? And what legacy do you want to leave behind?

You may, of course, be perfectly content with your life as it sits (but I assume you wouldn't be working through this book if that were the case) and if so, you might find this tricky.

You might also think of things such as 'quality time with my loved ones', which is perhaps an excellent indicator that the time currently spent with them isn't quality.

Regardless of your yearnings, this question is always very telling. Suddenly your priorities are on show ensuring the nagging voice of Whoville is harder to ignore.

What would you do if the end was near?

List four things that you'd want to do if you knew you had just six months to live:

1.

2.

3.

4.

Following on from the previous list . . . I am sure there are some things that flashed in to your head, but you immediately dismissed them because:
a) that costs far too much and I can't afford it, or
b) that takes so much time and you told me I only had six months.

Which brings me to this next list.

Let's pretend for a moment. Let's pretend you had extra money in the bank account and extra hours in the day and extra months in the year. Let's pretend that all of your responsibilities and obligations have been happily shelved for a period of a time.

What now? What would you love to do without those excuses?

Play piano? Write a book? Travel the world? Cultivate a gorgeous garden? Go back to school? Change careers? Have a child (or another one)? Get a pet? Move to another part of the country? Join a gym?

Get as creative as you like here. Really, really think about what you'd enjoy. Scary, isn't it?

It's actually quite easy to say, "Oh, I'd love to do XYZ but I just don't have the time because I work full-time and I'm raising kids." Or, "Oh, I'd really enjoy doing ABC but I can barely pay the bills, so I simply couldn't."

It's easy to blame life's circumstances, or other people, for limiting your options. However, if you do this for too long you may find yourself resenting other people (or life in general) for 'standing in the way' of your dreams.

The truth is, these excuses are just that: excuses. The internet and the library are both free and can provide you with (quite literally) all the knowledge in the world. Learning an instrument or hobby takes 10 minutes a day. A plant can be shared from a friend and planted for free. There are scholarships, online schooling, night school. The world is made up of flexible opportunities to allow for almost any situation.

So do you really want to do those things, and perhaps you're just scared? Or do you not want to actually do them at all?

We will get to those answers soon.

What if time or money weren't an issue?

List four things you'd do if you eliminated the excuses of time or money:

1.

2.

3.

4.

Whilst your imagination is firing, and you're thinking of all the possibilities unencumbered by reality, let's continue for a little while longer.

Consider, if you will, your perfect Average Day. Not a holiday, or a birthday, or a 'special' day. Just a day in your ideal life.

What does it feel like? What does it even smell like? I've given you a few pages here, so feel free to go in to detail.

What time do you wake up? What's your bedroom like, and how much sleep have you had?

When you wake, what's the first thing you do? Shower? Exercise? Read? Make a cup of tea? Spend time with a loved one?

When you have breakfast, what does your kitchen look like? What are you preparing? Or is someone preparing it for you?

Do you work? From home? Or an office? Or do you work outdoors? How many hours do you work? What sort of work is it?

Do you meet a friend for lunch? Or are you working on a fun side project during that time?

What time do you come home? Who is there? Family, partner, pets? Do you chat with a long-distance friend in the evening? Or watch TV? Go to the movies? Or read a book by a roaring open fire?

Do you stop in at your home studio before bed and spend an hour on your art, or craft, or hobby? Or do you take the dog for a walk around the block?

Remember, your idea of bliss is likely someone else's idea of misery—or vice versa—so don't think about what you 'should' be doing, just think about what you would love to be doing.

When you're done, have a little look. Is there much in there that is different from what you are doing now? Is your perfect life just a few tweaks away? Or is it vastly different to your current reality?

If there are many changes to be made, can you see how, in time, adjustments can be made to get you to this?

I first undertook this exercise when I was in my 20s—I wasn't married, I didn't have children. I thought it was an absolute fantasy, but I wrote it down anyway. I found that list not so long ago, and guess what? I'm there... and I realise now I should have been more specific (or perhaps it's just time for a new list)!

What does your perfect day look like?

In as much detail as possible, outline your ideal usual day: from the time you wake up, until the time you go to bed at night:

'Now' you've figured out what brings you joy. What lifts your spirit. What your dream day looks like.

Does it feel good? Do you feel a little lighter having established that you know what those things are?

No?

Maybe you're feeling like that dream life and those feelings of joy are a million miles away. That you're somehow even further away from a content and happy life than you thought when you started out.

You're not, I promise.

To prove my point, it's time for a stocktake.

As your brain races through all the many things you do on a daily basis that are not aligned with your new, exciting life, make a note of them here (under the 'nope' bit).

Your Perfect Day starts at 7am and you're currently climbing, bleary-eyed out of bed at 8am after a late night Netflix marathon and then rushing for the remainder of the day?

Your Perfect Day had you eating a healthy breakfast with a crossword puzzle, but you're standing at the kitchen bench downing a quick coffee while you scroll randomly on your phone?

Of course, it can't be all doom and gloom. Perhaps you love making new things for dinner each night and you're keen for that to be something that stays on in the future, so it featured in your Perfect Day. It's a definite Yep.

Maybe you have included a relaxing cup of tea in the morning and that's something you already do. So, tick—another Yep for you.

Revisit your lists from pages 43 and 63 and make some decisions about your life as it stands right now.

What needs to stay (yep), and what needs to go (nope).

What's working for you (& what's not)?

Looking back over this section, what elements in your life are getting you closer to joy (and what things are definitely not):

Yep:

Nope:

The other thing to check on, now you're familiar with the lists from pages 43 and 63, are those teeny, tiny adjustments you can make.

It's estimated that 40% of everything we do each day isn't a choice, it's a habit. I think we can all agree that once a habit is really ingrained in our lifestyle, it's super challenging to break. We're going to discuss decision making in the next section, but for now, have a look at how many things you do each day are undertaken out of autopilot. Each time you catch yourself going through the motions, consider what you could be doing instead.

Over time, small things can make a big difference. They're more realistic, less overwhelming and much easier to maintain than big changes.

Maybe your Perfect Day saw you without a cigarette, but you're currently on 10 a day. You might not be ready to go cold turkey, but perhaps slowly decreasing over time will get you there. Just a bit less for starters.

Maybe on your Perfect Day list you go for a 45 minute walk each day . . . and currently you're already doing half an hour. It's pretty easy to add an extra 15.

Perhaps by doing less scrolling, or watching TV, you can fit in more art, or reading, or learning that instrument you said you wanted to.

Less time at the gym might free you up to spend more time exercising outdoors, which is something that you've realised provides you with joy.

More of this, less of that.

What can you do more (or less) of?

Again, looking at your life right now compared to where you'd like to be, list a few things you can easily do more (or less) of:

More:

Less:

Part 4

How do you get what you want?

This next little nifty exercise is all about tricking your brain. After all, we all tend to swap between having absolutely no clue what we want . . . to thinking we know exactly what we want. We are actually often wrong in both instances.

A friend of mine was adamant she wanted a corporate job. She studied business at University, majored in accounting and economics and then went on to work for a global company. She was miserable. What she really wanted, she said, was to volunteer for a not-for-profit and work in a third world country.

Her thought process was incredibly complicated. She figured if she could just earn enough money to buy a place and be secure, then she could 'afford' to take a few years off, unpaid, and do her 'dream' job.

She could have headed directly into that role at any time, but she'd created a list of personal life rules that continued to limit her. As a side note, she now works in accounts for a not-for-profit and does loads of hands on work and is very fulfilled.

But back to you.

Let's assume that all your dreams have come true. You can literally have anything you ask for.

You now have your dream job, and it pays you your dream wage.

Then what?

Perhaps you want a brand new house. And a car.

Then what?

Well, now you've got the job, and the money, and the house, you might want to spend some time with the family. Maybe work less hours.

Then what?

Perhaps you'd like to learn how to sew, or paint, or restore classic cars.

Do you see where I'm headed here? This exercise might make it apparent that you don't need to get All The Things before you do The Other Things. You can actually do The Other Things now, if you like.

Funny that. Your turn.

What will come next?

When you have your perfect life, what will you do with your time/energy/money:

And then what?

And then what?

And then what?

And then what?

Did you know that we are not actually born with a natural ability to make decisions? Like reading and writing, it's a learned skill that improves with practice.

If you're one of those people who struggles with even small, everyday decisions, then it's a sign that you're decision-making muscle is weak. If you want to work on that, then start making as many decisions each day as possible. What to wear, what to eat, etc.

Of course, if you can't decide which shoes to wear to work each day, you might be thinking I'm crazy when I ask you to make a call on what your new life is going to look like.

Here's the awesome thing about this task ... I'm not going to hold you to it! It's just an exercise to put an option or two out there and wiggle around in it for a bit. Try it on for size and see how it feels.

How I want it to feel for you is light, joyful and just a little tingly-with-excitement. Mostly like a beautiful coat you've just added to your wardrobe at the start of winter, warm and cosy but also providing just enough sparkle that it makes you a little scared to leave the house in it ... no matter how much you love it.

That fear is completely normal. Doing anything new provides you with an element of hesitation, which is why it's the small steps and little changes that will lead you there.

But where, exactly, is there?

Have a play with Option 1. Where are you living and working? How are you spending your time? Where will this new life lead you? What are the pros and cons of this adventure?

If Option 1 all seems a bit much, then try Option 2. A few different choices, maybe less radical? Does that feel safer? Or does the thought of being where you are right now 10 years from now fill you with dread? Pros and cons again.

The final page allows you to blend your options, or add something new to the mix. Just keep going until you get the feeling right. Until you get the coat that you don't ever want to take off, even if people may notice you in it.

What does your new life look like?

Option 1:

Pros?

Cons?

What does your new life look like?

Option 2:

Pros?

Cons?

A final decision?

Take the elements from Option 1 and Option 2 that work for you, and come up with a final decision (for now, it doesn't have to be forever):

¶ If you've ever undertaken any sort of training (business or planning), you will have learnt about the concept of SMART Goals.

You see, just saying or thinking you want something isn't enough (sorry, it's not). You have to be clear. This will help your brain move forward and get the goal happening, even when you're not paying attention.

SMART is just a clever little acronym to help you remember, but essentially, for a goal to work it needs to be:

- Specific (get clear on what exactly what you want)

- Measurable (so you know when you've actually met the goal)

- Achievable (going to the moon isn't impossible, but there's more realistic, smaller goals you could undertake before that one)

- Relevant (random goals are unlikely and unhelpful, set ones that will get you to where you want to go, not just ones that sound cool)

- Timely (a reasonable time frame—3 months, 6 months, 1 year, 5 years—makes your goal more accessible. 10 or 20 year aspirations are great, and something to work towards... but as I keep saying, baby steps are much more realistic).

Here's the thing about writing down goals though: it works.

There's an urban legend about a 1950s Harvard (or in some cases, a 1970s Yale) goal study. Legend states that 3% of those in the study control more than 90% of the wealth, with their only common denominator being that the 3% wrote down their goals.

This elusive study has been found to not exist, but the popularity of the story lead to Dominican University undertaking their very own goal study. And guess what? Their results actually validated the legend. Writing down your goals offers commitment and accountability and helps you to achieve them.

Setting goals also tells your subconscious that you're actively making things happen, and it responds accordingly. More about that next, but first of all, let's set three, clear goals.

What would you most like to achieve?

What are your goals?

Goal #1 (remember to be specific, to be SMART):

How will you know you've achieved this goal?

Are you ready to tackle this goal, or do you need a smaller goal first?

Does this goal sit within your values, your plans for life and the ways you feel joy?

What's your time frame for completion?

What are your goals?

Goal #2 (remember to be specific):

How will you know you've achieved this goal?

Are you ready to tackle this goal, or do you need a smaller goal first?

Does this goal sit within your values, your plans for life and the ways you feel joy?

What's your time frame for completion?

What are your goals?

Goal #3 (remember to be specific):

How will you know you've achieved this goal?

Are you ready to tackle this goal, or do you need a smaller goal first?

Does this goal sit within your values, your plans for life and the ways you feel joy?

What's your time frame for completion?

Hey! Look! It's the last list! (Sort of, don't get technical on me. The ones on the next few pages don't count, they're different).

Chances are, you still have your doubts. It can't be that easy, after all. It's not like you just say what you want and it actually happens. Unless, of course, that's exactly what you do. Never know til you try, hey?

What will happen though, is this. Your subconscious is a powerful thing, and it doesn't actually know the difference between reality and imagination. If you're feeling the feelings, and you've informed your subconscious that this is the way forward, it will do its best to make it all happen for you.

Fancy elite sports coaches do exactly that—they have the player 'live' the game and when it comes to the real deal, their brain just knows what to do.

The small changes you undertake, the decisions and choices you make, will all add up to a life that looks an awful lot like the one you've hoped for. It's the awareness of it that's key.

Here's the thing: if you've just decided that you want to take a course in order to get a certain job that will provide you with the joy you're seeking, you're unlikely to agree to something that will send you in the total opposite direction (unless you're a total self-saboteur, and if that's the case, there are a few other books you need to read before this one).

The thing is, knowing who you are, what you enjoy, what you appreciate and where you are headed is a sure-fire way to find yourself living the sort of life that will make you happy.

If, in a year or two or ten, you find yourself seeking more, or something different, then perhaps it's time to start all over and read this book again. That's sort of the wonderful thing about being in charge of your own life. You get to decide.

For now though, I hope you're feeling like you have some direction and you're excited to move forward.

Have a think about what you can do today, or this week, that will move you forward with your goals and that wonderful new life. It doesn't have to be a big step, a little one will do.

What's a good first step?

One is good, two or three is better. What can you do right now to start working towards your new, exciting life?

1.

2.

3.

Part 5
Your resources

Quotes

Write down any sayings or quotes that resonate with you, those that remind you of who you really are:

Music

What songs make you feel happy, light or most like 'you'?
Write down the titles and artists here:

Films

List the movies that fill your spirit, or offer you such enjoyment you'd happily watch them over and over:

TV Shows

Name the TV programs you loved as a kid, and the ones you enjoy watching now:

Documentaries

Even if you're not a fan of documentaries, which 'real life' programs make you want to stop and pay attention? Which ones could you see yourself enjoying?

Books

List your favourite books, books you found easy to read, and books that others have recommended you read which sound interesting.

Articles

Fold and paste clippings, or write down web addresses for articles or sites that spark your interest.

Recipes

Write down recipes—childhood favourites, comfort foods or foods that make you happy.

People & Places

Which places have you visited in your life that really 'feel like home' and who are the people who fill your cup—the ones you love to be with? Include a why in both instances as a solid reminder.

Memories & Moments

List wonderful memories or moments from your past, or write down good things as they happen so you can revisit those experiences again.

Well, that's that then.

I've even provided extra pages just in case you want to write more things down (in fact, I encourage you to do just that).

The questions have ceased, the lists are complete. My one hope for you is that having undertaken these exercises you feel more confident in your You-ness.

These triggers, feelings, memories, reminders and desires all come together to build one unique Whoville (if you didn't read the intro you won't know what I'm on about here) that is just for You. Now your Whoville is recognisable and, most importantly, now you know it's there, you're less likely to ignore it.

All living things require love and water and you're no different. Be sure to nurture yourself as you would your very favourite friend. Speak kindly, always, and check in often to ensure joy is a regular experience. I think it was Snoopy who said we don't just have one life to live. We have one death, but we actually have a new life each and every day. Best to enjoy it, don't you think?

The more you lean in to your Whoville - the truth of who you are - the happier you will be and the easier your life will become. Going with the stream rather than fighting against it will always be a more agreeable option.

If you've found this mini journey of self discovery interesting and illuminating and it's resulted in you seeking more, here is one further list for you: authors, speakers and wise ones (living and dead) who have offered great insight. You might want to check them out next (and the ones you like will undoubtedly lead you to more).

Marcus Aurelius	Rumi
Florence Scovel Shinn	Alan Watts
Gabrielle Bernstein	Joe Dispenza
Pam Grout	Gaye Hendricks
Wayne Dyer	Gabor Mate
Eckhart Tolle	Michael Singer
Rhonda Byrne	Brene Brown

Happy living, and happy list making!

www.ingramcontent.com/pod-product-compliance
Lightning Source LLC
Chambersburg PA
CBHW040416100526
44588CB00022B/2845